We're from Brazil

Emma Lynch

Heinemann Library
Chicago, Illinois

Customer Service 888-454-2279
Visit our website at www.heinemannlibrary.com

Editorial: Jilly Attwood, Kate Bellamy, Adam Miller
Design: Ron Kamen and Celia Jones
Picture research: Maria Joannou, Erica Newbery
Photographer: Debbie Rowe
Production: Séverine Ribierre

Originated by Ambassador Litho Ltd
Printed and bound in China by South China Printing Company Ltd

09 08 07 06 05
10 9 8 7 6 5 4 3 2 1

Library of Congress Cataloging-in-Publication Data
Lynch, Emma.
   We're from Brazil / Emma Lynch.
      p. cm. -- (We're from ...)
   Includes bibliographical references and index.
   ISBN 1-4034-5802-2 (library branding-hardcover) -- ISBN 1-4034-5811-1 (pbk.)
   1. Children--Brazil--Juvenile literature. 2. Family--Brazil--Juvenile literature. 3. Brazil-
   -Social life and customs--Juvenile literature. I. Title. II. Series:
   F2510.L96 2005
   981.06'5--dc22

                              2005002614

Acknowledgements
The publishers would like to thank the following for permission to reproduce photographs:
Corbis pp. **29a** (Kevin Schafer), **30b**(Eye Ubiquitous/James Davis); Corbis p. **30c** (Wolfgang Kaehler); Harcourt Education Ltd pp. **5a**. **5b**. **6a**. **6b**. **7**. **8**. **9**, **10**, **11**, **12a**, **12b**, **13**, **14**, **15**, **16a**, **16b**, **17**, **18a**, **18b**, **19a**, **19b**, **20a**, **20b**, **21a**, **21b**, **22a**, **22b**, **23**, **24a**, **24b**, **25a**, **25b**, **26**, **27**, **28a**, **28b**, **29b**, **30a** (Debbie Rowe).

Cover photograph of Ingrid and her brother and sister reproduced with permission of Harcourt Education Ltd/Debbie Rowe.

Contents

Some words are shown in bold, **like this**. You can find out what they mean by looking in the glossary.

Where Is Brazil?

To learn more about Brazil, we meet three children who live there. Brazil is in South America. Brazil is the largest country in South America.

Key
- ● Capital city
- ▲ Mountain

COLOMBIA

Amazon River

AMAZONIA

BRAZIL

PERU

PACIFIC OCEAN

Brasília ●

BOLIVIA

0   250   500   750 miles

MINAS GERAIS

▲ Sugar Loaf Mountain

Iguaçu Falls

Rio de Janeiro

ATLANTIC OCEAN

North

W ─ E

S

NORTH AMERICA

EUROPE

ASIA

AFRICA

BRAZIL

SOUTH AMERICA

AUSTRALIA

▲ This is a map of Brazil. The capital city of Brazil is Brasília.

Brazil has many **plains**, hills, and mountains. The weather in Brazil is **tropical**. Brazil has a huge **rain forest**. The rain forest plants grow well in the tropical weather.

Most people in Brazil ▶ live in cities.

▼ The Amazon rain forest covers most of northern and central Brazil.

5

Meet Guilherme

Guilherme is six years old. He lives in Rio de Janeiro. Guilherme lives with his parents, sister, and grandparents. His father is a **publisher**. His mother runs a nursery school.

▼ Guilherme and his family like to go to the beach.

Guilherme's mother

Guilherme's father

Guilherme

Guilherme's sister

▼ Guilherme enjoys barbecues, but his favorite foods are **prawns** and cheese omelettes!

Guilherme's family sometimes have a barbecue. Guilherme likes eating fish and steak cooked on the barbecue.

Guilherme's Day

Guilherme goes to school five days a week. There are 20 children in his class. He studies math, English, art, Portuguese, and religion. Guilherme likes learning English.

▲ Guilherme's school is nearby so he can walk there.

At recess, Guilherme and his friends play soccer on the playground. When he gets home from school, Guilherme has to do an hour of homework.

Fun in Rio

Guilherme loves swimming and soccer. He lives near a very famous soccer stadium called the Maracanã. Guilherme wants to be a swimming teacher when he grows up.

◀ Guilherme supports Brazil's soccer team.

A big celebration called Carnaval takes place in February. Guilherme enjoys Carnaval! There are parades through the streets. People dress up and dance to **samba** music.

Soccer

Many Brazilian people love soccer. They call it *futebol*. Brazil's soccer team is very famous. They are the first team to have won the World Cup five times.

▲ People everywhere enjoy playing and watching soccer.

▼ Pelé played in the Maracanã
Stadium in Rio de Janeiro.

Pelé is known as one of the world's
best soccer players. He is from Brazil.
He played for soccer teams between
1956 and 1977. He scored more than
1,200 goals!

Meet Christian

Christian is seven years old. He lives in a village in Minas Gerais. Christian lives with his mother and father. Their village is small and everyone knows each other.

▼ Christian's grandparents live next door.

Christian's mother

Christian's grandparents

Christian

Christian's father

Christian's house has a garden and a cornfield where he can play. Many of Christian's relatives live near him. He likes to visit them.

15

Christian's School

Christian walks to school with his cousins. Christian has a lot of good friends at school. His best friends are Edgar and Tonineo.

▲ Christian lives near his school, so he can walk there.

Christian's teacher

There are 20 children in Christian's class. They study math, geography, Portuguese, history, science, and religion. Christian's favorite subject is science.

At Home

After school, Christian does his homework. Christian's mother and father both work at home. Christian's father makes bowls out of **soapstone**.

▼ When Christian grows up, he would like to make bowls too.

▼ Christian's mother **weaves** rugs in their home.

Christian's mother makes rugs. She sells them in the village. The family also grows most of the food they eat.

Landmarks

Brazil is a beautiful country with many landmarks to see. There are some huge waterfalls called the Iguaçu Falls. They are more than 2 miles (3 kilometers) wide!

▲ Many tourists visit these beautiful waterfalls.

This is the view from the top ▶
of Sugar Loaf Mountain.

Another famous place in Brazil is
Sugar Loaf Mountain. It has a statue
of Jesus on top. Tourists can go up the
mountain in a **cable car**.

Meet Ingrid

Ingrid is eight years old. She lives in Amazonia with her mother, father, brothers, and sister. They spend a lot of time outside. They work or play near the house.

Ingrid's mother

Ingrid's father

Ingrid's sister

Ingrid

Ingrid's brothers

▲ Ingrid's house is made of wood.

▼ Ingrid likes playing outside in the rain.

Amazonia is the area of land around the Amazon River. The weather there is very warm and rainy. Ingrid's village is a safe place to live, although there are many snakes!

Working Hard

Ingrid helps her mother and father with their work. Ingrid's mother works in the house. Ingrid helps her mother with her housework. She helps her by setting the table.

Ingrid helps wash the ▶ family's clothes, too.

▼ Ingrid enjoys watching her father get ready to go fishing.

Ingrid's father is a fisher. He brings fish home for the family to eat. Sometimes Ingrid helps him to get the boat ready.

School and Play

Ingrid goes to school five days a week. She enjoys studying Portuguese, but she does not like history! Ingrid wants to be a doctor when she grows up.

▲ After school, Ingrid does her homework for half an hour.

When Ingrid has free time, she likes to play with her friend Alime. Ingrid also likes to ride her bike around the village.

Nature and Wildlife

A lot of Brazil is covered in **rain forest**. There is rain forest all along the Amazon River. Many **rare** plants and animals live there.

▼ Brazil has many unusual trees and plants.

Many of the plants and animals in Amazonia are in danger. Large parts of the rain forest are being destroyed. Some people want to clear the land for farming or to sell the trees as **timber**.

Over 18,000 types ▶ of animal live in Amazonia!

Brazilian Fact File

Flag

Capital city

Brazilia

Money

Real

Religion
• About 80 percent of the people in Brazil are Roman Catholics.

Language
• Portuguese is the official language of Brazil, but people also speak Spanish, English, and French.

Try speaking Portuguese!
Olá .... *Hello.*
Cuidado .... *Take care.*
Muito obrigado / obrigada .... *Thank you very much.*

Glossary

cable car small car that moves along an overhead cable to take people up and down mountains

plain large, flat, grassy area of land with few trees

prawn shellfish that is like a shrimp

publisher someone who makes books

samba Brazilian dance

soapstone type of rock

rain forest thick forest of tall trees that grows in a hot, rainy place

rare something that there are not many of

tropical hot and muggy, with lots of rain

timber wood that is ready to be used for building

weave way of putting together threads to make a rug

More Books to Read

Auch, Alison. *Welcome to Brazil*. Minneapolis, Minn.: Compass Point Books, 2002.

Campos, Maria de Fatima. *A Child's Day in a Brazilian Village*. New York: Benchmark Books, 2001.

Fontes, Justine and Ron Fontes. *A to Z Brazil*. Danbury, Conn.: Children's Press, 2004.

Index